BOA
EDITIONS LTD

AND

AND

Poems by
MICHAEL BLUMENTHAL

AMERICAN POETS CONTINUUM SERIES, NO. 116

BOA EDITIONS, LTD. ❧ ROCHESTER, NY ❧ 2009

First Edition
09 10 11 12   7 6 5 4 3 2 1

For information about permission to reuse any material from this book please contact The Permissions Company at www.
permissionscompany.com or e-mail permdude@eclipse.net.

Publications by BOA Editions, Ltd.—a not-for-profit corporation under section 501 (c) (3) of the United States Internal Revenue
Code—are made possible with funds from a variety of sources, including public funds from the New York State Council on the Arts,
a state agency; the Literature Program of the National Endowment for the Arts; the County of Monroe, NY; the Lannan Founda-
tion for support of the Lannan Translations Selection Series; the Sonia Raiziss Giop Charitable Foundation; the Mary S. Mulligan
Charitable Trust; the Rochester Area Community Foundation; the Arts & Cultural Council for Greater Rochester; the Steeple-Jack
Fund; the Ames-Amzalak Memorial Trust in memory of Henry Ames, Semon Amzalak and Dan Amzalak; and contributions from
many individuals nationwide. See Colophon on page 112 for special individual acknowledgments.

Cover Design: Sandy Knight
Cover Art: "Portals" by Patricia Wilder
Interior Design and Composition: Richard Foerster
Manufacturing: McNaughton & Gunn
BOA Logo: Mirko

Library of Congress Cataloging-in-Publication Data

Blumenthal, Michael.
 And : poems / by Michael Blumenthal. — 1st ed.
   p. cm. — (American poets continuum series ; no. 116)
 ISBN 978–1–934414–21–7 (pbk. : alk. paper)
 I. Title.

PS3552.L849A8 2009
811'.54—dc22
                                    2008044325

BOA Editions, Ltd.
Nora A. Jones, Executive Director/Publisher
Thom Ward, Editor/Production
Peter Conners, Editor/Marketing
Glenn William, BOA Board Chair
A. Poulin, Jr., Founder (1938–1996)
250 North Goodman Street, Suite 306
Rochester, NY 14607
www.boaeditions.org

NATIONAL
ENDOWMENT
FOR THE ARTS
A great nation
deserves great art.

State of the Arts

NYSCA

for David and Kirsten Wellbery,
and in memory of John Mack

and with such friends…

And what you do not know is the only thing you know
And what you own is what you do not own
And where you are is where you are not.

—T.S. Eliot, "East Coker"

And (I) lie in the moonlight still wearing my raincoat…

—Lu Tung-Pin (fl. 870),
translation by Red Pine

CONTENTS

III. And Here I Am

IV. And So On

PROLOGUE

And

is a beautiful word, so underrated in the nomenclature of grief and desire.
Like its near-namesake, it can carry many times its own weight: Take:
I saw you, and, from the moment I did so, my life was never the same again,
or: *There was a residue of sadness in his face, and only when I looked him*
in the eyes could I see the hard luck that had befallen him. And accretes to itself
what it can, in its agglutinizing conduct and its lust for listmaking. *Grass*
lines the pond, writes Lei Chen, *and water lines the bank, the sun sinks*
in the mountains and in the icy ripples. Or my own: *It was a cold and wintry day*
and, as I walked out into it, I felt revivified and lucky to be alive, and full of joy.
Whew! you might say, that's a shitload of *and*'s to pack into a single sentence!
But *and* has its own priorities: It can even go, as it just did, next to a *but*
without significant damage. *And I was hungry, and tired, and my heart ached*
for a little womanly sympathy. And, of course, can simply introduce
the next thought, or the next item on a list, or suggest that there is more to the story,
and that whatever has been said thus far suffers from congenital incompleteness.
And this is what I wanted you to see, he said, wanting to divert attention
from his own conjunction, but he knew all along it was really the and
he had wanted her to hear, so that when he turned to her once more
at the theater, it was all but inevitable that he was going to say, as I say
to you now, friends, preparing to turn the page: *And listen to this…*

I. QUESTIONS, AND MORE QUESTIONS

And How Shall the Orchestrations of Night Love Us?
And How Shall Our Defeats Resound?

The stars twinkle and sputter to mark the transit of Venus.
But this too can mean little if we believe, as we must,
in the world's small and large lucubrations. A boy

poisons his own night with a curse, a girl on a skateboard
shakes her fist at the stars. Everyone has a rambunctious eye
on the future, a list of regrets for the past. The mockingbird,

who knows little of sounds that are wholly his own, dreams
of a world in which imitation is more than flattery, a pure
conviviality of sounds and utterances, not simply a mockery,

but a religion of sorts. *Of sorts*—ah, that's the rub! We are
out of sorts, in sorts, trying to sort out, each in his own way,
what sense there is to be made of a world where the planets roam,

the stars are extinguished before our very eyes, the sun seems
no more than a large bulb with a blackhead, and everything
we listen for in the deep of the night reminds us of something else,

of something we have heard before, or seen, or prayed towards,
as if a wandering planet could remake the world, or our mutterings
could all be turned to poetry, our sincerities overheard by some God.

And How Shall the Angels Dissolve? How Shall the Nights Prevail?

It may be there is nothing more monumental
than this mere shadow on the wall, dancing
as fast as it can, or that young boy, ecstatic

with how tall he has grown (though it's mere physics
and the reflection of light that have made him so),
examining his shape as he moves, shaking his head

towards the trees, becoming his own diptych
in the fading light, and he has not the slightest idea
how it will end for him, though he knows

that the air is rife with the anarchy of the possible,
that the hills are moving, ever so secretly, during
the night, and that even the ambergris of the whales,

floating somewhere in the sperm-rich Atlantic, will be
transformed eventually into an elegant perfume
for the idle rich, and that the female birds of Joan Míro,

those mysterious anthropomorphic shapes, will become
scrutable eventually, amid the bright clarity of some
inspired tomorrow, and that whatever possible singing

we are capable of, whatever Muse-ridden symphony, is never
entirely ours, but the property of the spirits, the night,
the harvest. And the deep, emblazoned rat-a-tat of the stars.

And What, Really, Is *'the Monotony of the Sublime'?*

Who knows if the angels hiding in the stairwell are really as bored
as they seem to be this Saturday morning, or if they have tired
of the large, Vesuvian possibilities of their lot and are embittered

by the monotony of it: the sublime riffraff they must contend with,
the filigreed banisters, summer air wafting through ventilators as if
it had nothing better to do than relieve the citizens of this world?

Who knows if they have not secreted themselves just to irritate us,
to suggest the quotidian is merely another kind of monastic order,
a plethora of holinesses gathered like strewn wildflowers that

have flowered for lack of choice as to what to do with themselves
and are now filled with the ennui of the uselessly beautiful,
nodding their heads like nuns scolding infidels, flaunting their habits,

shaking their fingers, trembling with every breeze, as if the papacy
of the clouds had been offended, as if all the secreted cardinals and
cross-dressing rabbis were ordinary taxpayers, hands cupped

under the stratosphere, asking for spare change, praising the generous
air, mumbling in so many tongues even the politicians are confused,
as if all the scenery of the earth had been painted a perfect gray.

And for What Is the Deliquescence of the Air?

Storms can happen in secret, they can sneak up on us, or else
they can be announced by the air, a gradual darkening of sky
then a quick shudder of life, a distant rumbling, a bold stroke

of lightning *et—voilà!*—there you have it: a world wet with
its own suggestions, wild to be turgid for no reason. Umbrellas
open, the raincoats come out from between their mothballs,

all the accumulated sins of inclemency gather under the eaves
to demonstrate their kinship with wetness and decadence, and I
know of no one who, on a torrid summer night, would refuse

the tempests and tornadoes, the hailstones, the uplifting winds
that can come in the wake of mere barometric change, as if
the earth itself had taken umbrage at some purely human error

and was now avenging itself, but remarkably so, with a tin-
tinnabulation of the stars, an efflorescence of stones, a dampness
throughout the phenomenal world that can only be seen as a

signpost of something greater, a portent of some future home,
a phantasmagoria of hope, an invitation to dance, everything
dissolving and dissolving, into water and branches and pure air.

And Who Shall Maintain the Luck-Strewn Bestiaries of the Hills? And Who Shall Discipline the Lakes?

A mere drizzle is no tragedy: you make for indoors and hold
your plans for the lake for another day. The hills hug and hoard
what little water there is, don't want to surrender their hegemony

over the hidden beasts and armadas of insects that occupy them,
creatures all eager to soak up what little moisture there is, urgent
to be wet, and the buzz and drip of summertime manages its little

symphonies of sound, assuring that no one will have everything
they hoped for, but no one nothing, nature's rough justice,
eschewing every possible abstraction, pitter-pattering, sending

a downflow of its excess gravitywards, everything calling out
center center, centripetal in its longings, and we who know so little
about the push and pull of the natural world, its accretions and

excretions, what else is there for us to do but accept the flow,
quake in our uncomfortable little shoes, and say our blessings
over the hills and lakes, so wild to be what they are, so immune?

And Whose Is the Triumph of Stinky Similitude?
And Where Is the Rapture of the Seas?

Everyone knows there is nothing sweeter than the scent
of a new morning, and, though the day it announces
may lead to disappointments and unplanned emergencies,

it is best to begin on a note of optimism, it is best to imagine
that only the good-hearted and gentle of spirit will triumph
and that it is not the candidate with the best smile who will

necessarily defeat the others, but he with the greatest purity
of soul, he most adept at conversing with the trees. Yes,
there is a bad scent in the air as evening converges, citizens

turn on their TV sets and are inundated with the slick, the
calculating, the studied sincerities of those for sale at a
low price, yet somewhere, slinking forward behind a bush,

there must be a Moses of possibilities, someone who can part
the seas without first bowing to a golden calf, and if he
should make himself manifest in my lifetime, I too will cast

my humble lot with that abeyance of cynicism, I too will remove
the nose plugs from my nose, the ear plugs from my ears,
I will set sail on the parted waters, I will sing to the waiting moon.

And Where Is the Bodhisattva of Our Longings? And How Shall We Find the Rectitude of Night?

The one who has woken up, the one who has disappeared, he who has
gone beyond all possible images, beyond, even, the power of words,
these are the ways the Buddha (beyond, even, hatred) is described

and who could but envy him, that little stranger in lotus position, that
mysterium tremendum of tranquility, so we breath deeply, mumble
our mantras into the afternoon, burn a little incense, console ourselves

with some amateur etymology (i.e., the root words of passion and
suffering are the same), and the mind's at rest, even if the body's
fidgety in its wetsuit of flesh and longing. Wisdom, after all, was only

a right religion away, you always knew you could quiet the sound
of one hand clapping for its lost counterpart. Ladies and gentlemen,
we are beleaguered no more by the itching of parts we have no

real use for, a bird in the hand can certainly leave a residue, but
it can also cure us of that longing for what's in the bush, we can seem
more centered in some fabulous place if only we'd stop behaving

like poets looking for justice in the wrong places (wrong tools, wrong
location, wrong world) and settle down to the here and now of the truly
possible: nightfall and morning after, sun in earnest, vanished stars.

And After an Earthquake of Such Magnitude, What Can Be Said About the Gods?

that they are possessed of a gigantic indifference to our small human
destinies, that we are no more than a gathering of leaf-cutter ants
in the forests of their peregrinations, that we are the Tinkertoys,

the LEGOs, the jungle gyms, and Erector Sets of their leisure activities,
that the earthquakes, the wars, the famines, and the ravages of illness
that surround us leave them supremely unaffected, that they are busy,

just like the rest of us, with their love affairs and betrayals and their
little economic crises, their balances of payments, their tax returns,
their automobile inspection deadlines, their standing in line for flu

vaccine and tickets to the World Series, that they are busy doing their
Christmas shopping, waiting for their clothes to dry in the laundromat,
that they do not love us as they should have, or even as they might.

And, in the Face of Such Suffering, What Else to Do But Go On?

There are heroic people in the world: they board planes and light out
for the afflicted regions, they do not merely write out checks or shake
their heads with the anesthetized masses to Christiane Amanpour, they

commiserate with their very bodies, right into the line of fire, right into
the detritus of bones and rotted flesh, right into the midriff of suffering,
and what else to do but admire them, admonish ourselves for our timidity

and trepidation, our besiegement with self-interest, our *afflictus* with the personal,
oh life of only one body oh self-seeking, self-aggrandizing, self-obsessed life
of narrowing borders, and we sit before the winter fires with our brie and our

Côte du Rhône and the warmed chill of gratitude in our spines that we have been
spared so huge a portion of the world's horrid misery, so much of its incalculable
arbitrariness, its randomness of tragedy, its unspeakable suffering: everywhere

ribs of children sticking into pure air, everywhere humped and bloody, like dead
birds in a parking lot after a tornado, our human brethren, everywhere we,
the fatted and the blessed, who can (or choose to) offer nothing beyond sympathy

and self-castigation, who hug our tangible, living loved ones to our side
and pray that whatever has happened to the rest of the world will never happen
to us—not here, dear God, not here, please say it will never happen here.

And If There Is Truly No Help for Us, Why Not, Then, Genuflect Towards the Stars?

No one who has ever given up hope on anything can truly know if he has
abandoned ship prematurely, before arriving at some paradisal island,
or if he was wise to do so, prescient as to the unluck that awaited him,

no one who has scanned the horizon from the overdeck, half mercurial
with a sense of danger, the other half wanting to sleep in a hammock
beneath the slivered moon, can say which of his many cautions are wise

and which simply worrisome, but he, too, must know it is a gambler's
destiny to be up on deck, eyes fixed on the horizon, and that the one
sure amulet of luck wisdom allows us is to genuflect up at the stars

whispering our Hail Marys and Holy Moseses as if there were no
tomorrow (though there may well be one). No one who has perused
the wild wisdom of yesterday can say for sure if the repetition compulsion

(a risky phrase to use in a poem!) is alive and well, or if a man gazing
through a telescope into the future can rectify his life, *no one*, friends,
can tell us, so it's best merely to allow each little Eden to crawl forward

out of its cubbyhole, to see the bumps on the horizon as spectacular fish
and sit at the table eating for all we are worth, prayer books opened
at random, Kiddish and Kaddish and candelabrum wild to alliterate

our woes and our worries, something still beating beneath them as if
the boat chugging towards the harbor were our boat, and, in the inlet,
so much we hoped for, with grace and with liberty and justice for all.

And Can Anyone Who's Been His Own Soporific for Very Long Truly Sing?

I don't know very much about the deep triumph of the lustful angels
or whether anyone who's been his own soporific for terribly long can
truly sing, but I *do* know that each day begins with its own blasphemies

and, no matter how beautifully Richard Tucker may have sung *Kol Nidre*,
there are vows that will always need to be broken, the little bird who lives
at the base of my voice is dying to warble his way into the light, and all

who have stopped and started their own burials to buy themselves flowers
know that there is nothing sadder than the dark uplift that comes from
seeing one's own face in the cave of beleaguerment, nothing can more

easily lead to one's own downfall than lust diminished, or the downtrodden
similitude that comes from too much sleeping. Yesterday, my hands perused
the back of my lovely's neck, my lips her ears, and I was divinely blessed,

just to be here, among the perambulations of weather and weariness. In the
bushes there were birds, and, in the trees, leaves preparing to fall earthwards
towards their next cycle of death and replenishment. The ground was muddy,

half-frozen, a kind of inclemency for shoes and those in a hurry. (I wasn't
in a hurry, though, so I kissed her neck again and again, dwelling on the
beauty of what she was, and wasn't.) Every little wrinkle and crevice, every

nook and its spacious opportunities for pleasure and playfulness, came to
my attention, and the nervous wren who tries nightly to keep me from sleep
kept still for a while, I could rest my head, without needing to sleep, between

her head and her shoulders, I could inhale her womanly scent, and all that
I knew about the bountiful world could be, for a moment at least, mine
and I could smile from the edge of the bed, fully awake, kissing and singing.

II. And Search for Beauty in the Mystery of Sky

And the Dark Has Encapsulated the Nighttime, and the Trees Are Gone

The moon was out last night, mysterious as ever,
Janus-faced, casting its light over the stubborn trees,
and when I went out, singing beneath the willow,

who else but the lucky owls, the inscrutable fox,
the secretive hedgehog, and the scototopic moles
would have seen me there, who else might have

known that I was singing to no one? Everything that
fruits and blossoms and cries out has its mysteries, even
the old plum with its prematurely rotted fruits, the fig

struggling to find sunlight against the wall, the apricot
that keeps me guessing year in and year out as to
its possible future—even they have no vision of the

afterlife that's any likelier than my own. Listen:
in the creeping dark, a bumblebee sleeps in its nest,
dreaming of honey; a reptile, a little garden snake

dozes beneath the stones and, when we all wake
in the morning, who will be any the wiser for what
the trees have whispered to themselves in our absence,

and who will have overheard me singing, and who
could have ventured even a guess that this is how it
would all end, that the sun would resurface again

to find only this, only this, and the trees in vain.

And the Spirit Has No Voice of Its Own, Yet the Spirit Must Sing

The two mourning doves doing their mating dance in the Jardin du Luxembourg,
what do they, really, know about love? Heads lowered, unaggressive,
they circle and dance, cooing wildly and squawking, pecking and retreating,

yet there is so little to say, really, when it comes to *amour*, we urge what we can
out of the resonant silence, the forced *tendresse*, the dress lifted passionately,
the beloved who does not answer despite our most fervent implorations. Oh sin

of sins! What could be better for us than to simply allow the voice to speak,
whenever it wishes, its little symphony of regrets and inadequacies? Bird calls,
the mating sounds of frogs, elliptical utterances of all kinds, and no one, not even

their maker, can say for sure what they mean, we only speak them into the stillness
to avoid our own awkwardness, branches distending towards the heavens, susurrus
of wind, mutterings of the drunken and deranged, and what was it I had just said

to you, right when we were interrupted by our own heavy breathing? Was it that
yes, I *had* loved you, sincerely so, and though you had never truly rewarded me
for my feelings, I was still committed to being here, in this beautiful park, saying

whatever comes to mind, in the botched language of the ravenous mouth, full
of good usage, of romantic equilibriums that can't find their equals, circling
and dancing, cooing and squawking and—oh yes—pecking and retreating.

And the Manic Energy of the Planets Shall Beckon to the Stars

Nothing more remarkable has ever smelled of the stars than this,
and who knows if Jupiter is really up there shining, or if it is
the bellicose North Star, or the transit of Venus, who knows

if meek little Pluto isn't off somewhere bathing in its plenitude,
whether Orion hasn't laid down its sword, and the big bear,
whatever its name is, has woken from its hibernation to rise,

swatting the galaxies? Angels have been spotted by reliable sources,
dressed in their sleepy gowns and long underwear, speaking
on cell phones, but only a few among the blessed truly know

what they are saying, can decode the hieroglyphic babble of divinity
and make sense of it, treating it like an ordinary dispatch, following
directions as serfs would on old world plantations. All the rest of us

can do is continue gazing up at the heavens, certain something is
happening we'll finally have use for, taking notes in any language
that comes, fighting back tears, sleepily nodding our way among the hills.

And the Small, Eclectic Hieroglyphs of Morning Shall Hide the Hills

The small bird chirping in the butterfly bush outside knows something
about the day I don't yet know. It's Wednesday, but feels like a weekend,
so maybe he's simply richer in feeling that in calendrical know-how, or

the worm he has just excavated is particularly delicious; in any event
the cat has her eye on him, she is circling the base of the tree, and my
heart, too, is a rat-a-tat of hopes this morning—why not?—for each day

is a new sun- or cloudrise of possibilities, the night's rain has re-inspired
the trees, every little creeping and crawling thing is making its way
to somewhere, the mail will arrive this afternoon, ravenous for readers,

and far off, within the cloudscape, the hills are having their secret conversations
with themselves, planning their day, orchestrating their mischief for the sake
of hikers, and not even the mystics know whether they are truly our friends

or if they have some secret agenda, whether amidst their powwows of hillocks
and mosquitoes some purely inhuman trouble is brewing that will, later,
surprise us with the dark complexion of the world at night, and its silly sleep.

And the Great Benevolence of the Eyes Is That They Can See

not just the white-tailed deer, the great blue heron, or the sharp-toothed muskrat,
but also the nervous little nuthatch, the titmouse, the red-eared sliders plunging
off logs back into the water, and the sweet flaming matchsticks of the cardinals.

Ah yes, the pleasure of the eyes is their attentive gaze as the woods grow luminous
with possibilities, full of motions arrested and unarrestable, outlines sharpened,
colors reconsidered (even by the color-blind). *Grass lines the pond and waterlines*

 the bank, wrote Lei Chen, *the sun sinks in the mountains and the icy ripples.* What
all he must have seen! And now the benevolence of leaf-fall has already passed,
chickadees dart up and about, and the squawking, shit-dropping Canada geese

and mallards perambulate beside the pond. *Everything can be encompassed
by a little inner quietude*, I've often thought to myself, *just as soon as the heart
stops beating for itself alone.* Then the eye gathers up the body's nervousness,

chagrin itself is reevaluated amid the God-scented loftiness of the great outdoors,
a squirrel buries its nuts, a dog follows its nose into the underbrush, Vesuvius
itself would refrain from erupting to consider these possibilities, and, Chanukah

be damned, I am slinking like a good, reticent goy through these woods,
my eyes have seen what my hands have done (and all the other body parts
as well), and, every time I look up, it seems that some god is calling to me

quietly quietly, feasting his own eyes on what I have wrought merely by
being here, merely by letting the rhapsodic light welcome my gaze,
reilluminating the beneficent universe, talking on key, calling me home.

And the Small, Cantilevered Emblems of the Hills May Be in Vain

Stillness has its own ethos: a bird, terrified, on
its branch, does not tell jokes. But the human world
is filled with farts and catcalls, with the bombast

of too many syllables uttered in vain, and how
shall we demonstrate to the hills that we are serious
in our self-importance, that we have been singing,

all these years, for the mere pleasure of listening
to our own voices? Slowly the river runs
between the beeches and oaks, the willow quivers

in the slightest of winds, and everywhere we look
something is beseeching us: *silence silence*
amid the deep, dismissive susurrus of the trees.

And These Are the Broken Syllables of the Luckless Hills. And This Is the Night.

No one who knows anything about ointments or orchestrations
or who lives daily for the glorious fuck that may yet come
his way (or the true love that won't) can say he has truly tried

giving his best efforts to what truly matters—No, no such person
can gesticulate towards his own paradise and hope that some bored
guide to the underworld will pause from his usual duties and point

out to him that he has strayed too far, that he has lost his way
on the roadmap that leads nowhere and has wound up here, in
this bloody ditch of used tires and resurrected guinea pigs, a man

surrounded by farm implements he has no idea how to use or where
to pawn for a better something, oh ladies and gentlemen of the jury,
please take your time, please allow yourselves all due deliberations,

remember that the burden of proof in cases such as these is nearly
insurmountable, that the prosecution must show beyond a reasonable
doubt that I, you, all of us, have strayed from a world of limited

possibilities, we have gone greedily into the meshwork of rapture,
we have chosen to cast our lot with the wing-scarred Icaruses
of the world, oblivious to their fathers, ever navigating upwards,

clack-clack-clacking like storks and perambulating on their lofty nests,
loving the mercenary night from high up in the hills, while all their little
siblings are gathered beneath the trees, burning and grazing, desperate to be.

And Here Is the Small, Damp Vesuvius of the Hills

No one really knows if the pasqueflower will have done its duty
by the time the soft mists and drizzles of April have arrived, or
whether the silly voices that resemble the small oracles of beasts

can truly speak to us, but I do know that, whatever way we dare
look at it, the perfect regard of some similitude looks back at us
from its posture of haughtiness, and, one angel after another,

the molecules of significance undress, the insects hang-glide
into the valleys, and everyone who knows anything about love
gives his own little demonstration of affection, the birds commence

nightly to pontificate from the bushes, the elixirs of the underbrush
rise and proclaim themselves, and *up up up* in the remarkable hills
the ardor for majesty takes off its clothes and the animals rise up

in their lairs, and every single-celled animal that knows how to pray
prays, the sunflowers sway in the valley, and the little child within us
says its prayers, and heads off to sleep, and the hills wink good night.

And the Academy of Exuberance Envelops the Trees

Anyone who has ever felt the lustful little angel that inhabits his body
knows how easily the day can get away from one: small vesicles
of blood and lymphatic fluids make their way brainward, and soon

everything that breathes and takes in light is dressed in the slinky
and transparent fabrics that just beg for kissing and removal. Watch
how quickly a young girl can undress when she thinks she's alone

near the banks of some river, or how everything that flesh touches,
some days, begs for additional sweetnesses, or at least an end
to the myopia of narrow dreaming. Maybe it was only an illusion,

the way the bark breathed and exhaled and told its story that day
in Canada, or how easily the Northern Pike made themselves manifest
in the luminous waters, really, it's hard to tell at times whether the

up up up of desire creates, or responds to, the world, but the end result
is always pleasure of some sort, the captivating susurrus of some bird
or the haloes of flesh, and any tree that can murmur "I love you," we

ought to remember, is worth listening to, as is the butterfly landing on
the butterfly bush, the owl hoo-hooing amid the branches, anything at
all to convince us we are not here in vain, and the trees that love us

and the remarkable orchestra of wind and strings that plays in our sleep.

And the World Has Its Own Conviviality, and Each Is Privy to His Own Singing

Small birds, with their voluptuary islands of mirth and singing,
must know something we're not sure of: they bristle and warble,
ruffling their feathers as if some unrelinquishing itch lived within

and, if they are nervous, it's only part of some larger nervousness
the universe itself must feel, decathlon of singing, Olympiad of
chatter and whistle. We ourselves are merely here: someone

better knows our God-given purpose, someone inscribes us
in books we've never read, will never have access to, and the plot,
with its meanderings of theme and purpose, remains a mystery.

Nonetheless, it's better to look up into the trees and pray: whether
our God's the Christian one, or Yahweh, or the omnipresent Buddha
of pantheistic leanings, in all likelihood, *someone's* listening, the same

mysterium tremendum that sent the birds. Each makes his own way
into whatever clarity he has access to, but, meanwhile, best to enjoy
the view, take in the décor of this room we've been invited into,

shape what small tintinnabulations of joy reach us from the treetops
into a song, whether or not love finally reaches us, whether or not
we can say that *this* is the way it is, or could be, or merely was.

And the Angel of Ointments Is Not a Salve

The pockmarked angel who visits you regularly
but failed to come to the party you so kindly gave for him
is now in the kitchen. He is waiting for some dark

escutcheon of beauty to manifest itself, perhaps while you
are out, perhaps even before the morning paper is delivered
and the day's news leaks out over the wires, purposeful

and beleaguered. He is waiting, but he waits patiently, pours
himself a cup of coffee, examines the art in the living room
and the false Persian carpets you've laid in the hallway,

admires himself in the bathroom mirror. This angel
has a rather bad complexion, but he is hardly
beyond beauty. He knows that a scarred thing

grows lovely as it heals, that the first cardinal
who comes to your feeder will depart before sunrise.
If there are monumental things to be done to your day,

he is prepared to do them: He's brought his tools.
But nothing, he knows, that ferments a life upwards
can be yours without a bit of exuberance. He's waiting,

hat in hand, a smile on his lips, and all he has
to offer up to you is a single prayer, a mystic thing
that dazzles in the dark and knows its way home.

And Up High There Are Apples, and Another World

Apples have come to me as if by some arboreal miracle
as have many other things, from up in the trees, on high
where the diasporic birds and the blue morpho butterflies

frolic so happily, and the arboreal monkeys, the flying
squirrels, and the crazy bromeliads with their aerial roots.
Frost said it would be good both going and coming back,

but if I were up there, not merely as a picker but a cohabitee,
it would take more than a little persuasion to get me down.
Why come back to earth, I ask, where love is such a botched

and perversely oriented thing, where little people are capable
of starting big wars, and virtue is no more than its own small
reward? Yesterday, I gazed up into the barrenness of January

and nonetheless there were red-throated sparrows, warblers,
an amazing flicker put-put-putting of its unipolar beak, and not
a creature in sight was on antidepressants or mired in its own

melancholy. I, grounded, was the one species incapable of
curing itself, and thought to myself: Up there, where the air's
clear, and there's no thought of the afterlife, *that's* where I'd

like to be. It isn't possible, of course, I know it, but there's no
harm done when a man, failing once again at love in midlife,
ponders the imponderables from down here, his feet firmly

on the ground, the taste of apples on his lips, nothing else to
turn to but what's on high, and unavailable, and what he craves.

And the Deep Elegy That Rises from the Mountains Has No Home

Wherever the girl who can abide no violence has slept
this night, I want to be there, encircled by her arms as if
I had no history but this one, praising the naked day

for its infinite possibilities and passion for rectification.
Surely in some ministry somewhere someone in power
is deliberating how best to cement his authority, and it

is only the weak of heart, or the truly resilient in spirit,
who can afford to pause and weep for the paltry ego
that resides there. It's the first of June, and every possible

cherry tree is blossoming forth, with only a random bird
and a poet with more time on his hands than he knows
what to do with to praise and feast on it. But let that not

be the issue here: The question, rather, is where that woman
sleeps and how to find her, and of all that has gone wrong
already and is likely to continue, and what bird shall triumph

by feasting on cherries, and who shall sleep with so imperfect
a peace in his heart, and who shall weep, and who shall be
comforted, and whose little rapture shall finally win the day.

"And a Man of the Way Doesn't Mourn Autumn"

Ch'eng Hao (1032–1085)

And why should he? The leaves, after all, are turning fabulous,
the air is revivifying in its freshness, girls are covering up
what it was only disconcerting to see, and a man might amuse

himself, as Wang Ch'i suggests, by teaching cranes to dance.
So why not? Everything, after all, grows luminous as it expires,
love survives its objects, the day its sunset, not even the faintest

swervings of the fickle heart have ever been recorded by the great
meteorologists, and the rain in Spain is not restricted to the plain,
or any other particular landscape, for that matter. Thanksgiving

is upon us, so why not believe in *this*, if we can believe in little else:
Rhapsodies can be heard in all kinds of different venues, the rubric
of the impossible, too, needs to find a home, not even the emperor

of ice cream is a true dictator, a little democracy stutters out from even
the tiniest of crevices, there is pumpkin pie for dessert, and all will be
well, everything will snucker along in its own way, and the dead birds

who were all bright and alive just yesterday will decorate our tables,
and the cranberries will be bright red, and the sweet potatoes will bear
only the slightest resemblance to their brothers, and we will lower

our heads to praise whatever there is to be praised. And we will eat.

And the World Is a Resilience of Hopes. And a Darkness as Well.

> *I will do nothing more to night tonight.*
> —Dan Chiasson, "One"

No one who has ever watched the sky for very long, with its
remarkable changes and its sweet little cacophonies of moods,
can help but know that tomorrow's weather, in all likelihood,

will bear little resemblance to today's, it will merely do its best
to humor us, keep us off guard, send us back and forth to our closets
for, first, a parka, then a wool sweater, then (damn it!) an umbrella

and the one thing that can truly be relied on is the unpredictability
of everything: susurrus and noise, thunderclaps and horrific heat,
inclemency and cure. Every channel you surf towards will provide

a different prognostication: Willard the Weatherman may smile
and act like a moron, but deep in his hip pocket, like a cable
from Baghdad, the bad news is waiting for us: low pressure areas

from the North, fault lines waiting to crack open in Asia, swirling
cones of tornadoes descending on us in Kansas. We can pray all
we want: the chemistry of currents and frontal systems has its own

logic. Only the birds, migrating and perambulating, know for sure
what uplift or downdraft awaits us, and even they are keeping it
to themselves, advocates of a Darwinian order. Keep all this under

your hat, if you are wiser than I am: You never know when you
might need it, and the person hurrying for the boat in front of you
could easily have been tripped up with a little withholding, he too

could have been dragged into the undertow, and not even the Pope,
in bed with the flu, could have saved him, no *corpus dei* for him,
no magic syllables, just rain and inclemency and a ladder to the stars.

And the Deep Abraxas of the Hills Shall Love You Too

Wherever you go they are there, the hills, shining in the distance
or on some other continent, but nonetheless wild to be worth our
attention, disarmed from all that's purposeful, and you, too, can go

to them, lift your arms from the day's task-ridden perplexities
and strike out *up up up up* until, like a terrestrial demigod, the
wildflowers splatter your gaze with their delectable fecundity.

You take on, slowly, the shape of your longings (and their possible
solutions), up into the air of your beloved beside you, and then,
rambunctious with all you lifted away from yourself, you mount

higher and higher, looking out over the blessed distance of every
vista, praising the ostensible fact of your own dissolution, a
spirit a stork a flamingo a pelican, you fill your beak with the fat

of all that is possible, you ride the updrafts and the currents, the ill
winds and the very good ones, and, when you descend once more,
a blessed nothingness will be yours, you will be in love, little angel,

with the groundedness of your own life, the wind that has sung
to you before will sing again, every perplexity shall be healed
in the deep air that ups and descends back into the breaking day.

"And the Fullfed Beast Shall Kick the Empty Pail"

T.S. Eliot, "Little Gidding"

Small birds that never amount to anything still have their way
of making us love them: they whistle and chatter in the trees
and when they mount each other, tenderly, among the leaves

they make only a little noise and fluff up their celebratory feathers
as if in answer to something we ourselves have no questions for.
Every little imp in a bush knows this: the day has its perfect hours

for lovemaking, and others that are good for, head down, searching
in the grass. Yesterday, I saw you in your red pants walking ahead
of me, and—whoosh!—there I was, a tanager among the pines,

all riled up and nervous with too many fluids. Silly girl, if, in
your little black underwear, you tempt me in the dark, imagine
what the light does to me, and how powerful *that* is. Truly,

I had nothing more to give you of myself last night than any man,
sated and avuncular and filled with his own good rhapsodies. But
one thing you can be certain of, nonetheless: the bird I saw there,

up in a tree from the village yard, was a happy bird, and the pail
I kicked, later on in the dark, bounced all the way up to heaven
and back, and it gave itself to the night, and was full, and slept.

III. AND HERE I AM

And I Have Known the Tedium of Playgrounds

And I have known the tedium of playgrounds—
the swing sets rising like suns into the blustery air,
the sandboxes alive with their own dust,

the jungle gyms climbed and risen through
and swung from by the monkeying offspring,
the ever-hopeful mothers in high heels and

the hopeless ones in their doughty aprons
and hairstyles of wind. I have seen the fathers
nervously gazing around, not quite knowing

what to do, and the innocent babysitters and au pairs
offering the fathers a new life, rekindling the fires
of youth. I have seen the children, morally free

and impervious to the happiness of their elders,
cackling like drunken chimps on the parallel bars,
hiding from and seeking their arthritic keepers,

and I have seen the day dismembered by noise
and graffitied child-yelps, I have sat here
on restless afternoons that might have been spent

amid the wet come-cries of older children. Yes,
I have known the tedium of playgrounds—
the children flying happily into the future,

the parents smoking and fidgeting, grounded forever.

And It Has All Come to Nothing, My Weeping and Railing

The world is.
Prairies pass—coneflowers, coquelicots, thistle.
And the passerine birds.

Whatever's monstrous stays monstrous,
and the beautiful, too—it stays.
So much wind

has passed through me,
so many invectives, blasphemies,
riffs and snatches of disputation.

And now I have come to see
it's all to no avail: I am
what I am, dreams be damned.

Only a true romantic
could hope to change me,
only something stronger than the wind is

could gather me up
take me in its arms
and blow me peacewards.

And Nanny Is Prayed for by a Pious Owl

I am the confessor of a coniferous time
and nanny is prayed for
by a pious owl.
     —Ewa Lipska, "That"

And nanny is prayed for, and we are prayed for, and everything under the sun
(and beneath the moon)—*they* too are prayed for, and why should it not be so?
Why shouldn't we pray, even if no one is listening, since the music of prayer is

the aperitif of longing, and my wife has just returned from washing the body of
a dead man in her hospice of departures, we should pray for him, we should pray
for every extinguished exuberance, and for every exuberance yet to be born, we

should pray for the riffraff and the aristocracy, and for the sweet nanny of everyone
who watches over us, and, when we are done with our prayers, we should allow
the voice its well-earned rest, we should sit quietly beneath the moon, allowing

what's blessed to be blessed, what's cursed to be cursed, we should no longer debate
the antithesis between free will and destiny, we should relish the singing, we should
lie in our beds, we should gaze up into the branches of nighttime and bless the owls.

And the Nomenclature of Love Contains a Sadness

for love is a bestiary,
I am sure of it, and
it, too, has a vocabulary

for the initiated only, with
an unmethodical grammar, a syntax
more Finno-Ugrian than European,

a complicated system
of suffixes and conjugations,
a mouthful of consonants

at every turn, and anyone
ambitious enough to speak it
will surely begin to weep

in a very short time,
there will be tears
running down their cheeks

and so many things left unsaid
without a syllable of their own
and without a dictionary

without, even, a register
or a system of punctuation
or a beautiful way of saying good-bye.

And I Will Cling to the Romance of Unattainable Love

for it is perfect
yet never to be perfected
and, though I am father to a young son,
and husband to a no-longer-young wife,
it is still the allure of that beckoning distance,
perhaps yet another incarnation of my long-dead mother,
that speaks to me, riveting me waywards,
sending me into another world than this one,
beckoning to me like a white handkerchief
or a yellow rose, riffling westwards
in the broken wind, just out of reach.

And I Never Before Loved Anyone As I Loved You

I could say it to you now, sincerely, but what good would it do me?
You have gone off to Rome, leaving only the sweet scent of your
orifices behind to console me. Never before did anyone so move me

with the sheer penumbral riffraff of their natural scent. And what
should I make of it now? Yesterday, there was a hedgehog in the yard,
the night before, a fox. Tomorrow the moles ravaging the begonias

will stutter, blindly, upwards from their little hills, desperate for the
underground, unable to swim in the hose's effluvia, and must I,
necessarily, feel guilt at having done what I needed to do? Certainly not,

you might say, you who are no more inspired by the culpable than day
by night, though you hardly deserve such equanimity, you of the unre-
ciprocating nerve endings and synapses, you of the static regard, you

whom I am missing now, but not nearly as much as I had supposed, justice
being my singular obsession, the lake cool, the mourning doves mourning,
and, above it all, the deliquescence of the air whispering its soothing song.

And This Unconventional Angel That Is Mine. And the World for Real.

Let me say at the very outset that it does not surprise me
that not all I have uttered to the hapless air has been returned
to me in kind, or that I am sitting here now, wound up

like a Russian doll with polemics and ideologies and the duff
and detritus of too many promises. Let me say I am tired
of the ineffectual ointments of the everyday, that the grass

has now been cut, the hedges trimmed, the children awakened
by the mower's hum, and last night's bee sting blown up
into a conspicuous bruise, a blemish not even a makeup artist

could disguise. *This is nature's way*, says my wife, who knows,
being a child of the natural, and my sister-in-law is screaming
at the children about too much computer time, the air's rife with

the scent of summer, flush and turgid with green, the forecast
is for thundershowers, a wind from the west, all to be followed
by birds, and the ratcheting harvest. And the night, then, for real.

And like Flies to the Odor of Shit, I to You

Never had I been so utterly lonely until I met you. I can say this now
in all sincerity, but how would it sound to the actually defeated, the
homeless, the abandoned with no such luxuries to complain about?

Certainly, no one ever was colder to anyone than you to me, but I
was *drawn* to you, after all, so what right do I have to whine about it?
Surely, no one ever argued that love is reasonable, or that a rational man,

aware of his own best interests, would engage in it, but let it suffice to
say that we are all, to a certain extent, ruled by instinct, and the mere
scent of you on the shores of Lake Balaton was enough to excite me

and leave me helpless. Now, though, that I've recovered enough of my
senses to speak, or simply fly off in a different direction, it's soothing
to a certain extent merely to say what I'm feeling, and to know you're

still out there, alluring to someone equally foolish as I was, someone
ripe to venture, nose first, into his own destiny, someone whose ship
is heading towards an iceberg, bearing no survivors, led by a captain

whose gaze is off in the wrong direction, who's had one too many
boilermakers and thinks he's in love: no life raft, and, surely, no sleep.

And I Got into the Car. And Drive, *I Said*

because it was America—yes, it was *Tennessee*—and the roads
were bloody humongous, the air resilient with leaf-fall and pollens
of all sort, around me everywhere were the beautiful sounds

of English, blessed English, *ma langue maternelle*, and I felt,
suddenly, more at home in my own country than ever before, yes,
it was the country of Buster Keaton and his namesake Diane, it was

the country of Bush and Kerry, Cheech and Chong, Groucho and
Zeppo, it was the country of Jimmy Durante, whose nose knew,
and of just-dead Rodney Dangerfield, who *couldn't* have been

a contender in any land but this, and it was the country, too, of my
dear friend John Mack, who believed that even the extraterrestrials
were welcome here, that even *they* could find some accommodation

and solace in this strange America to thee we sing, to thee, strange beast
of a country, I dedicate these lines, a wandering Jew who has wandered
back to the arms of his own country—so warm, so consoling, so filled

with these fabulous dissonances and ice creams, a place where even the
Red Sox can win the World Series, and someone is forever winding up,
forever releasing the ball, forever turning the bases, forever heading home.

And Now You Have Come to the Place in This Life
Where You'd Rather See a Monkey Than a Girl

Whether to stay up past your usual bedtime and wait for Melissa,
the gorgeous waitress at the *Mar Y Sol*, or to rise early in search
of the howler monkeys and the blue morpho butterflies, ah, *that*

is the question! Whether it is nobler in the mind to search out
endangered species, or to continue your usual preoccupations
with a proliferating one, is the issue, this night, that holds you,

vacillating as ever, yet somehow more centered, here in mid-age,
where little Melissa wiggles her tush beneath the plate of quesadillas
that's coming your way, right this very minute, along with a pitcher

of homemade sangria, and Billy the proprietor, slap-happy with
the money of *gringos* and *gringitas*, sends a knowing wink your way
and, a little full of monkey business yourself, you ask Melissa, *Te*

gusta bailar? And, yes, she *does* like to dance (would probably even
like to dance—and God knows what else!—with you,) but the gods
of sleep and of early morning are the ones you worship now, not

the gods of sex, not the lip-smacking orgiastic saints of your younger
years, and so you order a dessert of *trés leches*, leave Melissa a large tip,
wink at yourself in the mirror on the way out, and the monkey wins.

And the Last Sweet Flesh I Have Been with, It Was Yours

and it was in Budapest, in early summer, and the train had
just arrived at Keleti Station, and I took a cab (I was that hurried)
to your house, and you were still there, as you always had been,

still lovely, still unobtainable, still with that beautiful face of yours,
and the gap teeth, and that flesh so much younger than your years,
ah, yes, it was July, the same month we had begun in, years earlier,

and now July again, the cherries had already blossomed, the peaches
ripe, apricots impending, so much impending, but not us, we were
not impending, we were ending, we were finished, but for this, and

this was the epilogue, this was the tacked on, the sentimental, the ever-
futile epilogue, lubricated (even for me!) by booze, a cigarette, and then
the ever-beckoning, uncomfortable bed, my head squeegeed beneath

the headboard, your flesh (your ever-longed-for flesh!) all over me,
nostalgic for its own previous happiness, nocturnal as Chopin, sweet
as a *somloi galuska*, ripe as a ripe fig, creamy as cream itself. Oh, it

could have been such a lovely night. If only you had been there.

And the Self That Was My Old Self Is Still Within Me

But it is sleepy sleepy, has taken too many antibiotics, does not,
on occasion, recognize its own face in the mirror, yet still agrees
with Schopenhauer, that even this, the worst of all possible worlds,

doesn't exempt us from the obligation to put things beautifully,
that stylistic perfection, too, is a source of gratification. So what
if things are not the way they used to be, huge missteps taken

in every direction, wrong choices, unlikely alliances, friends
not in the highest places, but usually the lowest? The dogwoods
and Eastern redbuds, nonetheless, are flowering once more, I

have been poked and prodded for weeks, seeking to identify
the source of maladies and maledictions, and nothing whatsoever
has been found at the root of things, I am merely my old self

in an achier, sloppier version, en route to the usual destinies:
Zhivago, lumbago, back pain, angina—gaze shimmying towards
the obits, birds once identified now nameless in the trees, and all

I'm able to do about it is to keep calling my own name, listen
to András Schiff playing *The Goldberg Variations*, keep turning
my face towards the sun, waiting for someone, anyone, to call back.

And the Fraudulence of Surrealism Is Hereby Exposed

for a piece of cheese babbling in Swahili will never walk into your town,
nor will the anorexic pelican sequestered inside your wife's birthday cake
ever lecture you on existentialism and phenomenology, nor, for that matter

will the pitched somnambulance of the hills interrogate you regarding
your religious beliefs, sexual proclivities, and the like—no, nothing they
have tried to convince you of with their hilarious juxtapositions will ever

simply prove to have existed, nor will the girl in the bathing suit made of bananas
actually approach you on that Costa Rican beach, where the monkeys
are playing billiards in the trees and the sleek coatimundi that translates

impeccably from the Italian is, this very moment, running to catch a bus
before closing time at the casinos, no, none of this can ever truly happen,
but it is entertaining nonetheless, it is profoundly consoling to imagine

that you, with your mutually exclusive longings and appetites at odds
with one another, can still awaken in the middle of the night, go fetch
your King James Bible from the freezer, mumble a few of the Psalms

into the morning light, and some utterly tamed anaconda with the face
of a cardinal will slither down from the trees, rub its Bach-producing
fang against your cheek, and there, in the musically orgiastic resonance

of what you thought was merely another sunrise, a world will have opened
itself up to you, a universe of celestial perambulations and discordant harmonies,
a tangible Eden, filled with tenderness and spyware and delectable toads.

And Here, in the Old Synagogue on Hegedus Gyula Utca, I See Again My Father's Face

Budapest

for the old Jews are singing *En Kelohenu*, and they are chanting *ah ah men*
and he, so easily, could be among them here, he who is now ten years gone,
the old *tzaddik* of Washington Heights, the butcher's son, the failed cantor

who snuck into Karl Ehmer's on the East Side and gobbled down his ham,
the lover of goose fat and horseradish oh *father father father*, how little
I think of you any longer, as all sons must, yet I still carry you with me,

you old schlepper and davener, you walking bundle of sexual fury, you
who could sell milk to a cow, bagels to a baker, macaroons to a diabetic,
you old kisser of women's hands, you whistler in the halls, you lover

of Mario Lanza and Richard Tucker, you furrier to Rosalyn Tureck, you
worshipper of rabbis and cantors, you charmer of tollbooth attendants,
you bringer of Horn & Hardart's rice pudding and creamed spinach, you

overpowered by women all your life, you singer of "school days, school
days, dear old golden rule days," you lover of Asbach Uralt chocolates, you
in the ski parka on your honeymoon in Cortina d'Empezzo, you connoisseur

of boiled beef and calf's liver, baritone of "Du, Du liegst mir im Herzen,"
you who are standing in this synagogue now, davening and bowing, asking
for forgiveness, you with your bad breath and the stale smell of herring

and God's hand all ready to write you in his book once more.

And the Luck of One's Own Taxonomy.
And the Blessed Hieroglyphics of the Birds.

The silly woodpecker, peck-peck-pecking at the trees, does not speak
our language. Nor we his. To consider ourselves blessed by such lack
of communication requires a leap of faith, a hope for transcendence

hardly depending on words. Every day, birds leap from the trees, singing
in miraculous codes we do not understand and take, on pure faith, for
beauty. Perhaps, though, they are mocking us for our earthly complicity,

perhaps they know more about us than we think, and when we place our
heads upon our pillows, they gossip about us wildly in the perfect woods
trading little stories about our failures over worms and regurgitated fish.

Either way, though, twice daily I love you, and twice daily I celebrate the
magnificent little monument that is your body, even without their approval.
Up up up in the sky and trees, they swarm and follow each other, circles

and semicircles of perambulating wings and hoots, inscrutable semisignals
wafting between them like blissed sonograms of song, much the same way
that, when I whisper into your ear during the act, you arch upwards, birdlike,

making little noises only the other happy avians, I'm sure, can understand and
only the missionaries of flight would care to emulate and only the trees might
implore to come to rest and only the night can ease, and our busy little wings.

Everything Is Beautiful from a Distance, and So Are You

The young clarinetist, playing Mendelssohn's Sinfonia #10 in B-minor
in back of the orchestra may be exceedingly beautiful, it's hard to know
from here, just as I, to her, may be gorgeous myself and the day, in

retrospect, divine, as all the past loves of my life have been, and that boring
evening in County Derry as well, oh yes, they all are beautiful, now, when
I look back upon them, as, no doubt, my life will seem from some calm

and beautiful distance, some rapturous perspective, but here in the here
and now let me say that it's midafternoon, my lover is on her way over,
it's been a long chilly day in Budapest, what I thought was a herniated disc

is not, after all, a herniated disc, Mozart's 250th is behind us, as is the 60th
anniversary of Bartók's death, and it is only James Taylor on the stereo—
sweet, sentimental James—and I don't give a damn what anyone thinks

of my taste or emotional proclivities, I only know it's Thursday and in
an hour I'll be making love, and, looking up at me from the pillow,
my lover may or may not consider me beautiful, or even desirable,

but the deed will already be done, the evening before us, there
are roasted red peppers and goat cheese in the refrigerator, I'll be
as far from death as a man can be, oh can you imagine that?

And Here You Are

It's such a relief to see the woman you love walk out the door
some nights, for it's ten o'clock and you need your eight hours
of sleep, and one glass of wine has been more than enough

and, as for lust—well, you can live without it most days and you
are glad, too, that the Ukrainian masseuse you see every Wednesday
is not in love with you, and has no plans to be, for it's the pain

in your back you need relief from most, not that ambiguous itch,
and the wild successes of your peers no longer bother you
nor do your unresolved religious cravings nor the general injustice

of the world, no, there is very little that bothers you these days when
you turn, first, to the obituaries, second to the stock market, then,
after a long pause, to the book review, you are becoming a good citizen,

you do your morning exercises, count your accumulated blessings,
thank the Lord there's a trolley just outside your door your girlfriend
can take back home to her own bed and here you are it is morning you

are alone every little heartbeat is yours to cherish the future is on fire
with nothing but its own kindling and whatever it is that's burning
in its flames isn't you and now you will take a shower and this is it.

And No One Has Ever Had a Voice like This One.
And No One So Loveth the Earth.

Maybe you think there has never been anyone like me, and, if so, you're
certainly onto something, for, right beneath this sometimes joking voice,
resides a seriousness of purpose so sincere it would take a monarchy to

disarm it, a government so dedicated to its purposes every citizen seems
a hapless simpleton. Still, many a word has been offered by those with
little to add to the larger conversation, and I see no reason why I shouldn't

contribute my own two cents—after all, my words have been imprinted
between covers, and as I look up at the world that has been rendered to me,
I can't help but admire God's handiwork, shook foil and all, green with

protuberances. So let me sing my little song of praise, Ruby Dee, let me sing,
Ike & Tina, of myself and others, let me sing of the stupefying semblances
this world has to another, one we can only discern from this one, and how

even the insects, so numerous they could clearly overwhelm us, have a
sense of humility: they hide and dissemble, they buzz about, phototropic
and ravenous, with little else to do in their spare time but pester and sing,

make honey, pollinate the ravenous flowers, provide fodder for birds such as
the purple martin, who can eat 17 times its weight daily of the little pests,
oh let me tell you friends I have nothing to offer but praise and song, I speak

in the voice of one without mentors or imitators, I ascended, full-blown, from the head of the Muse, and I will not apologize, nor offer my regrets, simply because no one has a voice like this one, no one has taken the stage

so slyly and shyly, so filled with the mysterious symphonies of the birds.

IV. And So On

And There Was No More to Give to the World

God created the world in a mere six days
and, thinking he deserved it, rested
on the seventh. The animals were done,

the clouds, the paramecium had learned
to swim and divide, even the mockingbird
had mastered its repertoire, and, in the bayous

and swamps of Louisiana, the mix was ready
to welcome feud victims and alligators. Even
the warring factions of the future were prepared,

in their incipient hatreds, to kill and ravage,
and, though there was no Wailing Wall as yet,
the species was prepared, through tear ducts

and registers, all prearranged for davening,
to stand there shaking their heads and wailing.
No epidermis yet, but already pigments were lying

in wait to differentiate human from human, and
wide-bridged noses, high cheekbones, buttocks
and orifices all hungry for entry and confrontation

were latent in the evolving bird forms. No one yet knew
who would be president, or emperor for that matter,
or whether universal suffrage would provide the ultimate

be-all and end-all to every misfortune. Petunias
were already ravished for water, bean sprouts
and tofu aware of their nutritional futures, and lovers—

yes, lovers—already gathering on both sides
of Plato's homunculus for the right to reunite
with each other forever. Oh world! A mere six days

and all that already in place, like a chess match
in which pawns and soldiers were already lined up
but no move, yet, had been made. God knows

God, by then, was deserving of rest. And somewhere,
already lurking on the sidelines, the serpent
was preparing to strike, the apple to fall, and Adam

and Eve, still trapped inside a raptor or a fin-tailed
lizard, were preparing to find each other, so that God,
finally, could relax and enjoy his day, and see what a world

he had made, with what great entertainment, and
what dances, what magical, ongoing orchestrations
of pity and laughter, and, of course, what kinds of luck.

And a Girl Doesn't Smell like the Stars. Or the Bitter Trees.

The bingo of perpetual restlessness has little to say to a girl pinned
to the grass in the Parc des Buttes Chaumont by her boyfriend, why,
he is singing on top of her, inhaling the pure scent of romance and

there's nothing that's going to stop him now, after all it's spring and
last night was the Transit of Venus and so many birds are searching
for twigs on this lawn it could be a kind of avian prom, but he's got

her here, he's got her and he's not gonna give up until something good
happens, he's not gonna let her up until something calms him down,
why, it wasn't for nothing he bought this expensive bottle of Château

du Vendôme and those escargots, he's a man with a mission to pleasure,
he's an angel of possibilities, it's early summer and all the voluptuousness
of the world can be his for the asking, a Vesuvius of eruptions, a gaggle

of incipient happinesses, a rapture of ease-inflicted permutations, and he
is the only one in the world who knows it, he is master of all that is possible
here in this summer-specked park, with only the bitter trees calling his name.

And the Defeated Have Little to Offer Their Children.
And the World Sleeps On.

Because my son is sleeping so quietly, so peacefully, in the room next door,
I will not give up and mount a white flag on the doors of my house, I will not
partake of the noisy dreams of the defeated, nor will I mount on my doorposts

slanted prayers to some invisible god, I will not do anything but continue
as I have done, impervious to vicissitudes, anesthetized by rejection, insane
to make everything turn out right for the young and the innocent and the

resilient disciples of some better world than this. No, God, I will not stagger
like Sisyphus up his silly hill, I will not go on pushing my stones and boulders
on their way to nowhere. Delinquent on all my debts, I will continue to ride,

frictionless as a skateboarder, savage as a pit viper, remorseless as a serial killer,
on the highways and byways, these autobahns of lust and aphrodisia, serpent
to the stars, orangutan of the little trees, egg all over my face, and the sweet

mercurochrome of every possible healing applied to my wounds by the one
nurse in her white garments who can cure everything, sweet little amulet
of hope, sister of mercy, that uninhibited dancer who lets us praise and sleep.

And There Is So Much Ink in the World. And So Much Shit.

And on the Seventh Day, when he should have been resting,
God gave out paper and pen to everyone who asked for them,
(he was blessed with a generous spirit), and so didn't ask

too many questions about talent or inspiration, didn't bother
reading manuscripts or asking for letters of recommendation, no
it was a democracy of the eager and quasi-inspired, it was a good

place, even, to grab a little nooky on the side, an even better place
to hustle for influence, so what if most of it was going to turn out
to be utterly worthless, Auden, after all, was right: you could

respect everyone's right to play an instrument, but not necessarily
to be in the orchestra, meanwhile there was so much ink waiting
to be spent, so many trees to cut down, to hell with the screech owl

and the pileated woodpecker, there were stories that needed to be
told, every I crying out its I into the world, and God had faith in the
future, had faith in the aristocracy of the beautiful and the good,

he believed the apostle Paul had been right all along: that things
would take care of themselves; that, even amidst the noise, when
the perfect came, the partial would pass away, and be gone.

And Things Interfere with the Spirit. Yet the Spirit Sings.

Things can get you down. They don't deny the diasporic quality
of each blessing, how it seeks to reach under and out, spreading
over the landscape, hungry as a tornado, messianic as a settler,

but it, too, has its limits, and the spirit sags with the weight
of the purely human like a dropped torch, going out while it burns
leaving in its wake a scorched leaf, a burnt twig, a patch of

brown amid the green that reminds us even life's raptures have
their boundaries, little Switzerlands and Liechtensteins of the
possible. Yet we sing nonetheless, as if the voice were an empire

of its own, a Security Council of good intentions, a heliotropic bird
that knows enough about hope to be wise to the possibilities,
spreading its wings widely as if every taking off were a flight

into the possible, and we must dedicate to each within our parade
an anthem of sorts, cantata of diphthongs and countersongs,
procession of all that is possible so they, too, can sleep peacefully,

unaware of the dangers that lie ahead and lie here, that even the
slightest corrective asks us to go on, blasphemous as infidels,
wise as the bodhisattvas, still dancing and singing in our sleep.

And the Stupa of Zalaszántó Is a Vestibule of Peace

No one who has ever been to the Stupa of Zalaszántó can deny
that the Dalai Lama, too, has been here, and has blessed this site,
as he should rightly have done, for it is lovely, looking out

over the Lake Balaton valley, the Kali Basin, the firred hills
of Zalaszántó itself, and we who have come—Jews, Christians,
infidels—merely to picnic, should ask to be forgiven for killing,

before the very face of the Buddha, the stinging hornet that has
settled so peacefully on my ham sandwich, terrifying our son,
buzzing so musically, and if he, too, may be an incarnation

of the Buddha, it's good to acknowledge he might be merely
a hornet, whose sting can inflame, swell up, threaten the
life of its victim, so as my sandal rises into the Tibetan sky

of Western Hungary and comes down, flush, on the no longer
buzzing hornet, I can only hope that whatever encyclicals of peace
have risen from here will remain intact, every *Om* yet to issue

from me will be heard by Brahma, Vishnu, and Shiva himself, that
the peace of the earth shall not be threatened by the likes of me:
infidels, picnickers, sinners—their sandals rising into the air.

And the Whole Country Seems to Be Laughing. At God Only Knows What.

Clarksville, Tennessee

Jesus calls out to me from everywhere: *I am the way*, and who am I to doubt it,
especially when Oprah and David and Katie and Willard the Weatherman are
cracking their big smiles from every screen, and the whole country is cracking up,

yes, the whole country is yucking it up at jokes and comedians, in fact everyone
is a comedian: the President, the Democratic challenger, the mayors and
ex-mayors, yes, everyone is a comedian except for the reverend few who are

filled with such an excess of piety they can hardly smile, they are forever playing
Taps and reciting the national anthem, repeating "9/11" as if it were a mantra,
they are waving their flags in every possible wind, and even if they are not laughing

at Oprah and David and Katie and Willard, they nonetheless seem somehow allied,
it all seems like part of the same package of darkness and comedy, and, oh God,
how can it be that a man can come to feel so foreign in his own country, how can

it be that it seems impossible to pledge allegiance, more and more difficult to say
"with liberty and justice for all," or to sing, as my father did, "God bless
America, land that I love"? *Oh Lord oh Lord oh Lord oh Lord* you are everywhere

in this great country of ours and yet it can seem so terribly Godless to me, if you are
the way the light the life, why does it seem as if the darkness surrounds us, and why
are all these people laughing, and when (for God's sake, when) will they ever stop?

And the More Things Change…

after Roberto Calasso

Just as the rag with which Athena wiped Hephaestus' sperm
(described by the Greek poet Callimachus as "dew") from her thigh
fell on Attica, and landed in the earth mother Ge's womb, giving

birth to the monster-child Erichthonius, whose body ended in a
coiled snake's tail, so, too, our President's spilled seed landed
on a young girl's dress, giving birth to many different kinds of

snakes, moralists of all sorts, who, like the Athenian king Cecrops'
daughters, Aglaurus and Herse, couldn't resist peeking into the
offspring's chest, and were driven insane by what they saw. Still,

we must remember that all the Athenians were deeply devoted
to the seemingly monstrous child, seeing themselves in the Olym-
pian's unsatisfied desires, and that the snake-child Erichthonius

had the ability to restore life, and that, though his mother Athena
reared him alone, he later became King of Athens, and the temple
Erichthius was endowed with his name, and that whenever, to this

day, a man stands erect in the face of his enemies, he, too, is making
a claim to be descended from fire, and that Erichthonius went on to
marry Praxithea the nymph, and that they had a son, who turned out

to be more human, even, than his father, and far more human than the prurient girls, who jumped to their deaths, and who, had they lived, would have had only their own blood to wipe from their thighs: nothing

better, and surely nothing that could have given life, not even to snakes.

And the Army of the Separated Shall Drown in Tears

How many men have said good-bye to how many sons
and how many daughters at how many train stations
bus stations airline terminals how many men have gone

charging into the brink tear-stained and moving forward
how many of them have wept in their cars in the dark garages
or on the rain-swept buses from Gare de Lyon to Saint-Michel

how many gone back and vacuumed their empty apartments,
tossing out the Cracker Jack wrappers and Dr. Pepper cans
how many have folded the sheets for the next visit while scanning

the schedule of the evening's reruns how many have braved the
next morning, burying themselves in ambitions not really theirs how
many oh how many have gone on, bereft of their one unimpedible

meaning, ridden by guilt that should not be theirs, but for the innocent
faces of their children waving waving from the closing doors of the TGV
and Berkshire Transit and Long Island Railroad and Delta Shuttle

how many how many does it take to make an army a battalion an
industry for therapists and counselors and support groups how many
does it take in this world of doings and undoings this world of knots

tied and untied loves declared and undeclared, blood thinned out
by distance and separation and the sounds of trains leaving doors
closing engines revving buses parting oh Lord no man is an island

but we are an army an army charging eternally forward no enemy
in sight anywhere only love and more love and broken love and doors
opening and closing and our children waving *good-bye see you soon*

I had a wonderful time a wonderful time a wonderful wonderful time.

And Even the Ampleness of the Flesh...

Not even the buxom blond in a G-string sitting at the beach in Szigliget
can cure me of my melancholy this stifling day, not even her breasts
or her hidden triangulated vulva, not the oiled and salted skin she has

prepared so carefully, not her breath of mint, not her practiced fingers
or insatiable nose, not even the well-intentioned syllables of Hungarian
she sends my way, or her beckoning thighs, no, there is nothing at all

I am willing to submit myself to this unenraptured dusk, I am lonely
as a dwarf at a basketball game, desireless as a pope, and I can only say
to those who have come here to be with me that it will be a long night

without much in the way of diversions, advantageous to those who are
able to fast or to pray, or quick on their feet, but without solace for the
rest of us, and that when she gets up to leave, this blond, the world will

suddenly seem emptier without good reason, the grasses will lie down
before her departing feet like the wheat of the pharaohs, and only
the summer air will know for certain what she has wrought, and why

there was no comfort in her being here, and why even her absence is
incapable of diminishing me, I who have been here all day, singing
and praying, speaking to my only body of God only knows what.

And the Wages of Goodness Are Not Assured

for Aharon Appelfeld

That Jacob stole his own brother's blessing
and lived to triumph from it there can be
no doubt, or that Cain slew the gentle Abel

or that Job suffered so long amid the racked syllables
of his own believing, that the wages of goodness
are oblique and obscure, and not even assured

in some happy ending, all this should give pause
when we contemplate the abstract justice of
some perfecter world, when we sift through

the dark lexicon of possible deeds in search of
some glorious Eden where righteousness is a large
sequoia growing in a damp wood, surviving

drought and lightning storms, rising up over
the drone of its possible adversaries as if there
were no possible questioning its heavenly arriving,

as if the one recourse to an empire of darkness
were a purposeful upreaching, a shaft of light
that finds its way over the contentious canopy

of all that diminishes it. No, it may be better
to remember Juliek, playing his violin in the dank air
of Buchenwald, how he saw no other avenue

out of the ghostly enterprise than to keep playing,
to keep guiding the bow gently over the strings
while the dead were being heaped on the living

and the wages of goodness were being paid in
a dubious currency, when the only thing left
for a man to do was just keep playing like that

into the light of this darkening world.

And to All a Good Night

It's the bottom of the ninth inning and it doesn't matter, really, who's winning
or who will suffer the humiliation of making the final out. The pitchers are tired,
the bats weigh heavily on the shoulders of their batters, and even the coaches,

elliptical with wet palms and tongues and ready-to-wipe hands, are dreaming
of the night's first martini, when all that will matter are the generosities (or
lack thereof) of their wives, whether the tuition at various second-rate colleges

is paid, and if the future of the strike zone is something they can truly count on,
or if it, too, is subject to revision, and, with it, their prospects as managers. Oh,
Larry Doby, Enos Slaughter, pinch hitters young and old, where are you now?

And the pretty girls, ravenous outside the clubhouses, how could they know
of the steroids and illicit activities of their favorite pin-ups? The Hall of Fame
is filled with the deviant and unrepentant: they practice their swings, retired

on vast pensions, in underwear their forbears could only have dreamt of, coveted
from safe distances. Ah, stars, the future is yours, all atwinkle in the night sky
above domed stadiums. Rain and every possible inclemency can no longer enter,

fair weather has been declared a necessity, the spittle of pitchers unhealthy for everyone,
and if, as the clouds disperse, the roof is lifted and a bit of fresh air allowed in, let it be
done at the flick of a switch, without undue commotion, and let the birds now gathered

on the fiberglass roof find another venue to bear their young from, let the old coaches
gather again before their fires, and let every pinch hitter in the on-deck circle come up
with a game-winning hit, let this be a blessed year for all, and to all a good night.

And the Elegant Etcetera That Knows No End

in memory of Joseph Brodsky

A sentence can go on and on: the *and*'s and *etcetera*'s of the world
unite in their garrulous splendor, extending our thought beyond
the margins and their original appetites. "And etcetera etcetera

etcetera etcetera," went the Russian, and who was to stop him?
Silly to think we are at the mercy of commas and periods, sillier,
even, to think a rambunctious mind can be stopped at the borders

of logic and sense. Every little effluvium wants to find its way
over the dikes created to contain it. Somewhere, in some New Orleans
of the mind, right this minute, the floodgates are opening, words

are swimming for safety, structures are being ravaged, and a man
who seems too small for all he is uttering, nervously maneuvering
a cigarette between his lips, is showing us the way to some new

linguistic nation, he is summoning every little *and* and *etcetera*
at his disposal, he is writing in a language not really his own, he
is widening his lips and out comes that Slavic tongue, murmuring

and and and etcetera etcetera please don't make me stop oh please don't

And the Cantilevered Inference Shall Hold the Day

Things are not as they seem: the innuendo of everything makes
itself felt and trembles towards meanings we never intuited
or dreamed. Take, for example, how a warbler, perched on a

mere branch, can kidnap the day from its tediums and send us
heavenwards, or how, held up by nothing we really see, our
spirits soar and then, in a mysterious series of twists and turns,

come to a safe landing in a field, encircled by greenery. Nothing
I can say to you here can possibly convince you that a man
as unreliable as I have been can smuggle in truths between tercets

and quatrains on scraps of paper, but the world as we know
is full of surprises, and the likelihood that here, in the shape
of this very bird, redemption awaits us should not be dismissed

so easily. Each year, days swivel and diminish along their inscrutable
axes, then lengthen again until we are bathed in light we were not
prepared for. Last night, lying in bed with nothing to hold onto

but myself, I gazed at the emptiness beside me and saw there, in the
shape of absence, something so sweet and deliberate I called it *darling*.
No one who encrusticates (I made that up!) his silliness in a bowl,

waiting for sanctity, can ever know how lovely playfulness can be,
and, that said, let me wish you a Merry One (or Chanukah if you
prefer), and may whatever holds you up stay forever beneath you,

and may the robin find many a worm, and our cruelties abate,
and may you be well and happy and full of mischief as I am,
and may all your nothings, too, hold something up and sing.

And the World, After All, Is a Good and Gentle Place

it needs nonetheless be said, despite all that is contained in it, despite all
so many are doing to prove it otherwise, every day the sun rises and sets,
the clouds go on with their heavenly meanderings, the amazing riffraff

of the underbrush continues with its fermenting and fertilizing, oh dear God,
there is little choice, in the end, but to celebrate, to gaze upwards and consider the
amazing tintinnabulation of decoys and camouflages, this hardly-to-be-believed

cornucopia of fragrances and visual miracles, these stunning conflagrations that
rekindle the undergrowth, the capuchin monkeys and lemurs and the miraculous
little fish called *pumpkinseed*, oh wondrous illuminations of light and texture,

stupendous duff and detritus of dreams and hopes, ratatouille of delights, snippets
of conversation, ebullience of laughter, droplets of tears and sexual fluids, asters
pushing their way through the topsoil, bird dung and octopus dung, human and cow

shit as well and the sometimes heavenly scent of them, paprika and persimmons,
ginger and the snaps made from them that can form the crust on cheesecake,
cheesecake itself (the chocolated and strawberried varieties, the plain and lemony)

oh birds and all you little animals oh lice in my hair oh pontifical creeds uttered
from the Vatican and ridiculous fatwas uttered from the Moslem capitals oh
disputatious Israelis and Palestinians, why not look up, all of you, why not stop

for a minute to praise whatever there is in your line of vision: the Wailing Wall
and the freshly-dug tomb of Arafat, the little hybrid (bloodlines from God-knows-
where) girl nursing at the tit of her fear-stricken mother, the unfortunate young boy

raising his arm to throw a stone who might still be taught better, oh raptors
and honeybees oh ruby-throated and emerald-throated hummingbirds oh slug
that is climbing up, this very minute, my bathroom wall, I am not Whitman

but nonetheless I praise you all, I sing of myself and I sing of you and I am
fifty-five years old and my life, like everyone else's, is no paradise, but it
is good, and the sun is shining outside this window, and the splotched

illuminations of the ordinary should bring us peace, and the troops in Iraq
should be called home, and kindness allowed to prevail, not just abstractly,
and the blessed air in the trees will take us in its arms and say good night.

21 / "And What, Really, *Is* 'the Monotony of the Sublime'?": The phrase 'the monotony of the sublime' is taken from Philip Roth.

67 / "And I Got into the Car. And *Drive*, I Said": *Ma langue maternelle* means "my mother tongue" in French.

72 / "And Here, in the Old Synagogue on Hegedus Gyula Utca, I See Again My Father's Face": "Du, Du liegst mir im Herzen" is an old sentimental German love song whose title means "You, you dwell in my heart."

87 / "And the Stupa of Zalaszántó Is a Vestibule of Peace": A stupa is a dome-shaped Buddhist shrine. Zalaszántó is a small, remote rural town in Western Hungary, not far from Lake Balaton.

90 / "And the More Things Change…": The poem is inspired by the retelling of the original myth in Roberto Calasso's *The Marriage of Cadmus and Harmony* (Knopf, 1993).

93 / "And the Ampleness of the Flesh Cannot Cure Everything": Szigliget is a picturesque, small village along the shores of Hungary's Lake Balaton, and very popular, particularly in summer, with Hungarian artists and the Budapest middle class, as well as German and Austrian tourists.

Acknowledgments

The author wishes to thank the following periodicals, in which some of the poems have appeared, occasionally in slightly different forms:

Chattahoochee Review: "'And a Man of the Way Doesn't Mourn Autumn'," "And a Girl doesn't Smell like the Stars. Or the Bitter Trees";

Five A.M.: "And Now You Have Come to the Place in This Life Where You'd Rather See a Monkey Than a Girl";

Green Mountains Review: "And I Got into the Car. And *Drive*, I Said," "And the Whole Country Seems to Be Laughing. At God Only Knows What.";

The Hopkins Review: "And the Army of the Separated Shall Drown in Tears," "And the Deep Elegy That Rises from The Mountains Has No Home";

Legal Studies Forum: "And the Angel of Ointments Is Not a Salve";

Maggid (Israel): "And Here, in the Old Synagogue on Hegedus Gyula Utca, I See Again My Father's Face";

The Nation: "And the Wages of Goodness Are Not Assured";

The New Republic: "And Even the Ampleness of the Flesh…";

The New Yorker: "And Here You Are" (as "Here You Are");

Poetry East: "And Up High There Are Apples, and Another World," "And the Cantilevered Inference Shall Hold the Day";

Poetry Northwest: "And How Shall the Angels Dissolve? How Shall the Nights Prevail?"

The Poetry Porch: "And I Have Known the Tedium of Playgrounds," "And This Unconventional Angel That Is Mine. And the World for Real.," And the World Is a Resilience of Hopes. And a Darkness as Well," "And the Small, Damp Vesuvius of the Hills";

Salamagundi: "And the Fullfed Beast Shall Kick the Empty Pail";

The Southern Review: "And What, Really, *Is* 'the Monotony of the Sublime'?," "And Who Shall Maintain the Luck-Strewn Bestiaries of the Hills? And Who Shall Discipline the Lakes?," "And, in the Face of Such Suffering, What Else to Do But Go On?";

The Yalobusha Review: "And the Fraudulence of Surrealism Is Hereby Exposed," "And Nanny Is Prayed for by a Pious Owl";

Zone 3: "And After an Earthquake of Such Magnitude, What Can Be Said About the Gods?," "And It Has All Come to Nothing, My Weeping and Railing," "And the Dark Has Encapsulated the Nighttime, and the Trees Are Gone," "And I Will Cling to the Romance of Unattainable Love";

"And the Wages of Goodness Are Not Assured" was previously published, in a slightly different version, in *The Wages of Goodness* (University of Missouri Press, 1992).

My deep gratitude to the Literature Program of the National Endowment for the Arts for a Fellowship in Poetry for the year 2005–2006, which was of great help in the completion and revision of this manuscript.

I also wish to thank my wife Isabelle and my son Noah for teaching me, despite a certain resistance on my part, what love is—a lesson no number of poems in this world can adequately testify to, or repay. Everything I write is, directly or indirectly, for them, and part of an effort to deserve the goodness and grace that they have brought into my life. And to all the kind and hardworking people at BOA—especially to Thom Ward, for his intelligent and most helpful suggestions about the manuscript—my deepest gratitude, and my abiding friendship. My profound thanks also to C.K. Williams for his kindness, generosity, and friendship.

About the Author

Michael Blumenthal graduated from Cornell Law School in 1974 and was formerly Director of Creative Writing at Harvard, where he taught from 1983–1993. He is the author six previous volumes of poetry and the novel, *Weinstock Among the Dying*, which won the Harold U. Ribelow Prize for the best Jewish novel of the year in 1994 and has just been reissued in paperback. He has also published a collection of essays from Central Europe, entitled *When History Enters the House* (1998) and the memoir *All My Mothers and Fathers* (HarperCollins, 2002), about growing up in a German-speaking family of Holocaust refugees in New York. A frequent translator from the German, French, and Hungarian, he has published a volume of translations from the work of the Hungarian poet Péter Kántor and edited an anthology of poems about marriage, *To Woo & To Wed* (Poseidon, 1992). After teaching at universities in Hungary, Israel, Germany, and France, and practicing psychotherapy in Europe, he presently holds the Darden Endowed Chair in Creative Writing at Old Dominion University in Virginia and, in Spring 2009, will hold the Copenhaver Distinguished Visiting Chair at West Virginia University College of Law. He spends summers in his small village house near Lake Balaton in Hungary, and spent the month of May 2007 in South Africa working with orphaned infant chacma baboons at the C.A.R.E. Foundation.

BOA Editions, Ltd.
American Poets Continuum Series

Colophon

AND, poems by Michael Blumenthal,
is set in Adobe Garamond, a digital font designed in 1989 by Robert Slimbach (1956–) based on
the French Renaissance roman types of Claude Garamond (ca. 1480–1561) and
the italics of Robert Granjon (1513–1589).

The publication of this book is made possible, in part,
by the special support of the following individuals:

Anonymous • Lawrence Belle
Alan & Nancy Cameros • Gwen & Gary Conners
Peter & Suzanne Durant • Pete & Bev French
Judy & Dane Gordon • Kip & Debby Hale
Peter & Robin Hursh • Bob & Willy Hursh
Nora A. Jones • X. J. & Dorothy M. Kennedy
Jack & Gail Langerak • Rosemary & Lewis Lloyd
John Edward Lovenheim & Barbara Pitlick Lovenheim Charitable Trust
Donna M. Marbach • Daniel M. Meyers, *in honor of Robert Hursh*
Elissa & Ernie Orlando • Paul & Andrea Rubery
Steven O. Russell & Phyllis Rifkin-Russell • Vicki & Richard Schwartz
George & Bonnie Wallace • Pat & Mike Wilder
Glenn & Helen William